# THIS BOOK BELONGS TO

Name: Eddie     Age: 16

Favourite player: Pascal Strijk

# 2021/2022

## My Predictions...          Actual...

Leeds United's final position:

| 13th | |
|---|---|

Leeds United's top scorer:

| Raphinha | |
|---|---|

Premier League winners:

| Man City | |
|---|---|

Premier League top scorer:

| Mo Salah | |
|---|---|

FA Cup winners:

| Spurs | |
|---|---|

EFL Cup winners:

| Chelsea | |
|---|---|

Contributors: Peter Rogers

# A TWOCAN PUBLICATION

©2021. Published by twocan under licence from Leeds United Football Club.

ISBN: 978-1-913362-96-6

£10

# CONTENTS

## 01 ILLAN MESLIER

**POSITION:** Goalkeeper

**DOB:** 02/03/2000

**COUNTRY:** France

Illan Meslier has firmly established himself as Leeds United's first-choice goalkeeper following his 2019 arrival from Lorient.

The Frenchman kept eleven clean sheets as the Whites enjoyed an impressive return to the Premier League in 2020/21. Ahead of the 2021/22 season, Meslier signed a new contract at Elland Road committing his future to the club until the summer of 2026.

## 02 LUKE AYLING

**POSITION:** Defender

**DOB:** 25/08/1991

**COUNTRY:** England

One of so many players at Elland Road who has blossomed under the guidance of Marcelo Bielsa, right-back Luke Ayling enjoyed an ever-present 2020/21 campaign at Premier League level.

Having joined Leeds United from Bristol City back in 2016, Ayling is closing in on a double century of appearances for Leeds United. He began the new 2021/22 campaign with a wonder-strike against Manchester United at Old Trafford.

# 2021/22 SQUAD

## 03 JUNIOR FIRPO

**POSITION:** Defender

**DOB:** 22/08/1996

**COUNTRY:** Spain

Attacking left-back Junior Firpo agreed a summer 2021 switch from Barcelona to Elland Road.

Having began his career with Real Betis, 25-year-old Firpo moved to Barcelona in August 2019 and was a Copa del Ray winner in 2020/21. His move to Elland Road has been viewed as a real coup for Leeds United, with the player making his Premier League debut on the opening day of the 2021/22 campaign.

The side-foot pass is one of the most accurate passing techniques over shorter distances. The ability to find one of your teammates with a pass, even when under severe pressure, and retain possession of the ball is an essential factor in the way the game is played today.

# SIDE-FOOT PASS

# SOCCER SKILLS

## EXERCISE ONE

Set up a 10 x 10m grid. In one corner there are two players and on each of the other three corners there is one player.

Player A starts with the ball. Each player must pass the ball round the square in sequence then follow their pass. A passes to B then runs after his pass and takes up B's starting position. B passes to C and follows his pass to take C's position, and so on. All of the players must control the ball then pass it with the inside of their foot.

### Key Factors

1. Non-kicking foot alongside the ball.
2. Pass with the inside of the foot.
3. Strike through the middle of the ball.
4. Keep your eyes on the ball and your head steady.

## EXERCISE TWO

The set up is the same as exercise one.

In this exercise the players pass the ball in sequence, A through to D, but do not follow their pass, remaining stationary.

As soon as A plays the first pass, E sets off racing around the outside of the starting point. The players must pass the ball as quickly and accurately as possible while under pressure from E, who cannot tackle but is effectively racing the ball round the square.

The same key factors apply in this exercise as in the first, but the players are required to be able to pass the ball accurately while under pressure.

Any team who can retain possession through good accurate passing will always make it very difficult for the opposition. The side-foot pass is one of the most accurate passing techniques.

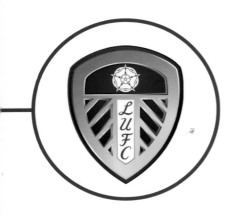

**Goalkeeper Nigel Martyn was an inspired signing by then Leeds United boss Howard Wilkinson.**

Martyn had already become the country's first £1M goalkeeper when he joined Crystal Palace from Bristol Rovers and when Leeds swooped for the stopper's services in 1996, the £2.25M move from Selhurst Park to Elland Road set another record fee for a goalkeeper.

Martyn played 207 Premier League matches for Leeds United and produced many match-winning performances, however it was his performances in Leeds United's European campaigns that won him so many admirers. A Man of the Match performance against AS Roma in the 1999/2000 UEFA Cup was followed by highly impressive displays in the Champions League a season later as Leeds reached the semi-final stage.

# LUFC HEROES

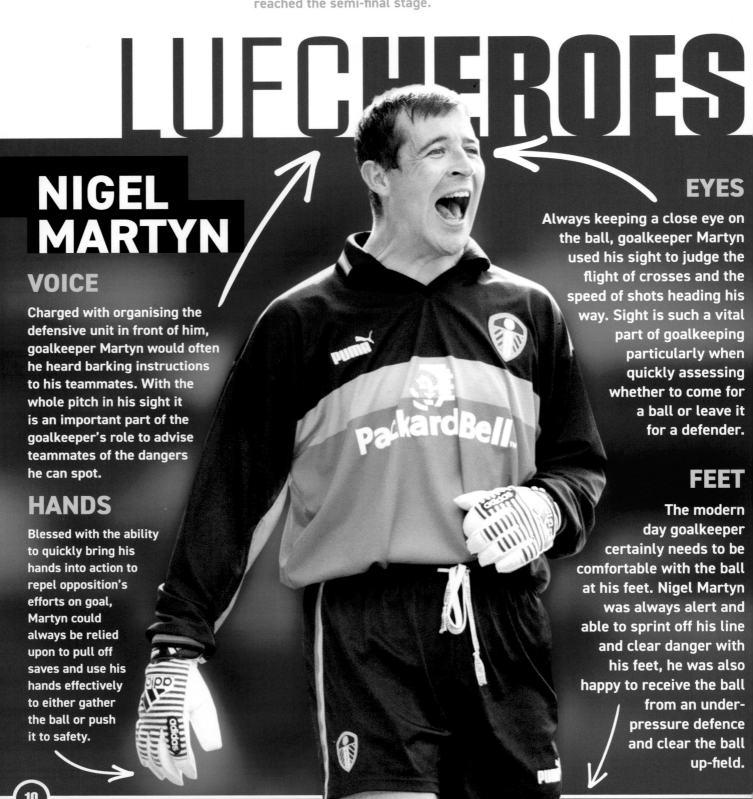

# NIGEL MARTYN

## VOICE

Charged with organising the defensive unit in front of him, goalkeeper Martyn would often he heard barking instructions to his teammates. With the whole pitch in his sight it is an important part of the goalkeeper's role to advise teammates of the dangers he can spot.

## HANDS

Blessed with the ability to quickly bring his hands into action to repel opposition's efforts on goal, Martyn could always be relied upon to pull off saves and use his hands effectively to either gather the ball or push it to safety.

## EYES

Always keeping a close eye on the ball, goalkeeper Martyn used his sight to judge the flight of crosses and the speed of shots heading his way. Sight is such a vital part of goalkeeping particularly when quickly assessing whether to come for a ball or leave it for a defender.

## FEET

The modern day goalkeeper certainly needs to be comfortable with the ball at his feet. Nigel Martyn was always alert and able to sprint off his line and clear danger with his feet, he was also happy to receive the ball from an under-pressure defence and clear the ball up-field.

| | | | | | | | | | | | | | | | | | |
|---|---|---|---|---|---|---|---|---|---|---|---|---|---|---|---|---|---|
| A | G | F | G | O | L | D | E | N | G | O | A | L | A | A | V | C | U | R | B |
| O | C | L | E | A | N | S | H | E | E | T | N | T | X | O | A | S | A | E | V |
| D | R | I | B | B | L | I | N | G | A | Y | H | B | L | U | C | A | T | M | I |
| E | B | P | H | R | N | R | U | T | F | F | Y | U | R | C | V | N | S | O | F |
| A | F | F | H | I | T | T | H | E | W | O | O | D | W | O | R | K | M | J | G |
| D | I | L | C | E | N | S | X | D | T | V | R | C | G | R | G | E | O | T | S |
| B | M | A | D | J | P | Z | E | U | I | W | J | F | N | E | A | D | E | Z | M |
| A | R | P | K | U | L | I | E | F | S | B | M | A | M | P | I | K | O | S | R |
| L | Q | A | T | A | T | M | S | D | O | E | M | T | R | P | J | P | Q | P | A |
| L | Y | V | C | P | O | A | G | O | I | D | U | A | A | I | Y | T | N | B | I |
| S | I | W | U | E | T | G | T | A | R | N | V | B | T | K | A | H | V | W | N |
| P | R | C | L | I | N | I | C | A | L | F | I | N | I | S | H | E | R | N | B |
| E | R | Z | N | S | T | C | H | X | M | A | M | A | M | I | E | N | L | A | O |
| C | Q | E | H | C | N | S | H | Y | O | S | U | J | G | L | T | U | E | M | W |
| I | O | A | F | O | S | P | T | E | W | R | O | D | B | Z | A | M | X | T | K |
| A | J | I | N | F | O | X | I | N | T | H | E | B | O | X | B | F | E | I |
| L | K | A | D | E | A | N | T | Y | V | N | R | K | B | S | Q | I | C | G | C |
| I | M | G | F | M | U | G | I | A | N | T | K | I | L | L | I | N | G | R | K |
| S | X | P | B | U | H | E | L | G | L | O | R | T | N | O | C | L | L | A | B |
| T | H | E | B | E | A | U | T | I | F | U | L | G | A | M | E | S | P | T | T |

# SOCCER SEARCH

Ball Control ✓

Bicycle Kick

Boot it ✓

Brace ✓

Clean Sheet ✓

Clinical Finisher ✓

Cruyff Turn ✓

Cup-tied ✓

Dead-ball Specialist ✓

Dribbling ✓

Flip Flap ✓

Fox in the Box ✓

Gaffer ✓

Giant-killing ✓

Golden Goal ✓

Hard Man ✓

Hit the Woodwork ✓

Magic Sponge ✓

Man On ✓

Nutmeg ✓

Rainbow Kick ✓

Skipper ✓

Target Man ✓

The Beautiful Game ✓

Treble ✓

ANSWERS ON PAGE 62

## 04 ADAM FORSHAW

**POSITION:** Midfielder

**DOB:** 08/10/1991

**COUNTRY:** England

**Adam Forshaw joined Leeds United from Middlesbrough during the 2018 January transfer window.**

Following many impressive performances in 2018/19, Forshaw continued his good form in Leeds' excellent start to their 2019/20 title success. Sadly after featuring in seven Championship matches at the start of the season, he suffered a hip injury which eventually required surgery in the USA. Everyone was delighted to see the midfielder return to first team action for the first time in nearly two years in August 2021.

## 05 ROBIN KOCH

**POSITION:** Defender

**DOB:** 17/07/1996

**COUNTRY:** Germany

**A full German international, central defender Robin Koch joined the ranks at Elland Road ahead of the club's 2020/21 Premier League return.**

A competent ball-playing central defender, Koch was signed from Bundesliga club SC Freiburg and made his Leeds debut in the thrilling opening-day match away to Liverpool. The former Eintracht Trier and Kaiserslautern defender featured in 17 Premier League fixtures last season as Leeds United sealed a ninth-place finish.

# 2021/22 SQUAD

## 06 LIAM COOPER

**POSITION:** Defender

**DOB:** 30/08/1991

**COUNTRY:** Scotland

Captain Liam Cooper was a key performer as Leeds United won the Championship title in 2019/20 and then proceeded to really make their mark at Premier League level last season.

A bargain £600,000 signing from Chesterfield in 2014, Cooper made 25 Premier League appearances in 2020/21 and then joined up with the Scotland squad for the Euro 2020 finals.

There are five Lucas the Kop Cats hiding in the crowd as LUFC fans celebrate reaching the Champions League in May 2000 as the team finished third in the Premier League. Can you find him?

# CLASSIC FANTASTIC

# DESIGN A KIT

**Have a go at creating next season's home kit for Leeds United!**

PHINHA

17

# 1973/74

Leeds United's all-white playing strip has been a long-held tradition at Elland Road. However, excitement and anticipation still surrounds the launch of every new Leeds United kit.

Each and every playing strip forms its own part of Leeds United history and supporters young and old will all have their own favourites.

Let's take a look back at four of the best...

Kit supplier Admiral produced a host of great Leeds United kits throughout the majority of the 1970s. In 1973/74, as the club landed the First Division title for the final time under Don Revie, they wore a crisp all-white shirt with a large white collar. In an era before shirt sponsorship became commonplace, the front of the shirt just housed the manufacturer's motif and club crest on the chest area.

A pair of no-nonsense all-white shorts carried just the manufacturer's logo and combined with the all-white socks, produced a look that was just pure Leeds United.

## DRESSED TO IMPRESS

A Leeds United team packed with Elland Road legends and managed by the great Don Revie were crowned First Division champions for the second time in six seasons when they landed the title in 1973/74.

The side made a flying start to the season, winning their opening seven league fixtures and remaining unbeaten until they suffered a 3-2 defeat away to Stoke City in February 1974. They lost just four league games all season and took the title ahead of runners-up Liverpool with a five-point cushion.

## HE WORE IT WELL

A phenomenal Leeds United marksman, striker Mick Jones netted 111 goals in 312 appearances for the club in an Elland Road career that spanned between 1967 and 1974.

He topped the scoring charts in the club's 1973/74 title triumph with 17 goals, 14 of which came in the First Division and included a brace in the 4-1 victory over West Ham United at Elland Road in November 1973.

The club launched a new kit in the summer of 1990 following promotion back to the old First Division and wore the same strip for the next two seasons - although there was a change of club sponsor for 1991/92 with the Yorkshire Evening Post replacing Top Man.

A classic all-white shirt had a round neck, buttoned blue collar with white trim - this theme was also used on the cuffs. The club crest, manufacturer's motif and sponsor's logo were all displayed in the traditional format on the chest area.

The white shorts had a blue trim at the bottom with a thin blue and yellow stripe on the side panels. The club crest and Umbro logo were displayed on the front of the shorts and the all-white socks were topped with a blue and yellow patterned band which had the Umbro motif woven into the fabric.

## DRESSED TO IMPRESS

After enjoying an excellent 1990/91 season when the side finished fourth in their first season back in the top flight, Leeds United proceeded to land the title in 1991/92, pipping Manchester United to top spot by four points.

Howard Wilkinson's men lost just four league games all season and the mid-season signing of Eric Cantona proved a vital final ingredient in the title success.

## HE WORE IT WELL

Lee Chapman formed an excellent little and large strike partnership with Rod Wallace in Leeds' 1991/92 First Division title-winning campaign.

Manager Howard Wilkinson's decision to bring Chapman to Elland Road in a £400,000 deal from Nottingham Forest in January 1990 certainly proved an inspired move - the experienced frontman scored 20 goals for the club in 1991/92, of which 16 came in the league success.

# 1991/92

# ALL KITTED OUT

# 2021/22 SQUAD

## 09 PATRICK BAMFORD

**POSITION:** Forward

**DOB:** 05/09/1993

**COUNTRY:** England

After topping the Elland Road scoring charts in Leeds United's 2019/20 Championship title-winning campaign, forward Patrick Bamford wasted little time in making his mark on the Premier League.

The ace marksman netted 17 Premier League goals as Marcelo Bielsa's men secured an impressive ninth-place finish following their return to the top flight. Among Bamford's 17-goal haul last season was a memorable hat-trick in the 3-0 victory away to Aston Villa in October 2020.

## 10 RAPHINHA

**POSITION:** Midfielder

**DOB:** 14/12/1996

**COUNTRY:** Brazil

Another exciting arrival at Elland Road following the club's return to the Premier League, Brazilian winger Raphinha joined the Whites from French club Rennes in October 2020.

He marked only his second start for Leeds with the only goal of the game to secure victory away to Everton in November 2020. He ended an impressive debut campaign at the club with six Premier League goals.

**Keeping fit and healthy is vital for all of us. So if you play footy for the school team or your local club, being fit and ready for action is sure to help you enjoy the game and perform to your very best.**

For the players at Leeds United, showing peak levels of fitness is essential if they want to feature in Marcelo Bielsa's team. Before anyone can think of pulling on the famous white shirt and taking to the pitch at Elland Road on a Saturday afternoon, they will have had to perform well in training at Thorp Arch and to have shown the manager, his coaches and fitness staff that they are fully fit and ready for the physical challenges that await them on a matchday.

Regardless of whether training takes place at the training ground or at the stadium, the players' fitness remains an all-important factor.

Of course, time spent working on training drills and playing small-sided games will help a player's fitness, but there is lots of work undertaken just to ensure maximum levels of fitness are reached. Away from the training pitches the professional players will spend a great deal of time in the gymnasium partaking in their own personal workouts. Bikes, treadmills and weights will all form part of helping the players reach and maintain a top level of fitness.

**Over the course of a week the players will take part in many warm-up and aerobic sessions and even complete yoga and pilates classes to help with core strength and general fitness. The strength and conditioning coaches at the club work tirelessly to do all they can to make sure that the Leeds United players you see in action on a matchday really are fighting fit for footy!**

# GET FIT FOR FOOTY

It has been said that dribbling is a dying art. The pace of the modern game makes it more difficult, but there are players about, even in today's lightning fast conditions, who have the confidence to keep hold of the ball and take on defenders.

# DRIBBLING
# SOCCERSKILLS

## EXERCISE ONE

As a warm-up exercise, players A and B each dribble a ball around a 20 x 10m grid, avoiding each other, but staying within the grid boundary lines.

They progress to a 'cat and mouse' race between the corners - the player with the most visits to each corner wins the race. One of the main problems in this exercise is avoiding the other player, and their ball.

## EXERCISE TWO

Now for a more realistic exercise. Six players are used as shown, with three attackers and three defenders at any one time. When play starts, the players with the ball attack any of the three opposing goals, changing their target as they choose. The defenders have, simply, to stop their opposite number from scoring, but must not interfere with any other pair.

## Key Factors

1. Close control.
2. Quick change of direction.
3. Acceleration away from defender.
4. Feints, to wrong-foot defender.
5. Head up to see the whole picture.

When the defenders win possession, they become the attackers, and go for goal themselves. This can be a very enjoyable practice, but also quite tiring.

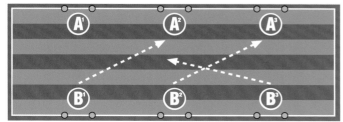

**1** Newcastle United ANSWER

**2** Wigan Athletic ANSWER

**3** Burnley ANSWER

**4** Charlton ANSWER

**5** Coventry City ANSWER

# GUESS

## THE CLUB

**6**

AFC Wimbledon

**7**

Liverpool

**8**

Millwall

**9**

Wolves

**10**

Nottingham Forest

Each football holds the clues to the identity of a Premier League or Football League club, how quickly can you solve them?

ANSWERS ON PAGE 62

# 2021/22 SQUAD

## 11 TYLER ROBERTS

**POSITION:** Forward

**DOB:** 12/01/1999

**COUNTRY:** Wales

Having joined Leeds United from West Bromwich Albion in the 2018 January transfer window, Tyler Roberts was another member of the Leeds squad to really make his mark at Premier League level in 2020/21.

Featuring in 27 top-flight fixtures last season Roberts netted his first Premier League goal in the 2-0 win away to Southampton in May 2021. His club form saw him included in Wales' 26-man squad for the Euro 2020 finals.

## 13 KRISTOFFER KLAESSON

**POSITION:** Goalkeeper

**DOB:** 27/11/2000

**COUNTRY:** Norway

Leeds United completed the signing of highly-rated Norway U21 international goalkeeper Kristoffer Klaesson in July 2021.

Capped at international level all the way through the various youth age groups, the 'keeper joined from Norwegian club Valerenga where his reputation has grown and grown with a number of impressive performances. Klaesson provides both cover and competition for the No1 spot at Elland Road.

## 14 DIEGO LLORENTE

**POSITION:** Defender

**DOB:** 16/08/1993

**COUNTRY:** Spain

A classy right-rooted defender whose comfort on the ball also allows him to operate as a defensive midfielder, Diego Llorente joined Leeds United at the start of the 2020/21 season.

Signed from Real Sociedad, Llorente made his Premier League debut against Chelsea and scored his first goal in Leeds colours in the 1-1 draw with Liverpool at Elland Road in April 2021. The former Real Madrid man has won eight full caps for Spain.

# PLAYER
## OF THE YEAR

## STUART DALLAS

**Northern Ireland international Stuart Dallas was the big winner at the Leeds United Player of the Year awards following the club's excellent season back in the Premier League.**

As the 2020/21 awards were handed out, Dallas landed a cool hat-trick of accolades following an outstanding campaign for the Whites.

Dallas was crowned the club's Player of the Year, ending Pablo Hernandez's three-year reign of winning the award. Then, for a second season in a row, the 30-year-old was named the Players' Player of the Year - whilst he also picked up the Goal of the Season award for his memorable late winner against Manchester City at the Etihad Stadium in April.

Now one of the longest-serving players at the club, having joined from Brentford back in 2015, Dallas was ever-present in Leeds United's 2020/21 Premier League campaign and also chipped in with eight vital goals.

Under head coach Marcelo Bielsa, Dallas has flourished playing in a variety of positions across the team and all at Elland Road were delighted when he agreed a new contract with the club in July 2021. The popular and well-respected Irishman penned a three-year deal, keeping him at Leeds United until the summer of 2024.

The 30-year-old is now closing in on 250 appearances for Leeds United. He has also won over half a century of caps for Northern Ireland and captained his country in their international matches against Malta and Ukraine in the summer of 2021.

## YOUNG PLAYER OF THE YEAR
# ILLAN MESLIER

**Goalkeeper Illan Meslier was named the club's Young Player of the Year for 2020/21 after a fantastic season between the sticks, making numerous vital saves and keeping eleven clean sheets.**

Having joined the club in August 2019, Meslier had to bide his time for an opportunity to shine in 2019/20. However, after keeping seven clean sheets in ten Championship fixtures towards the end of Leeds' title-winning campaign, he was in pole position to establish himself as the team's first choice 'keeper for 2020/21.

**The young Frenchman missed just three Premier League games last season and is sure to be one of the first names on head coach Marcelo Bielsa's team sheet in 2021/22 as Leeds United look to go again in the Premier League.**

A powerful Australian international striker, Mark Viduka was a £6M signing from Celtic in the summer of 2000 who went on to score 72 goals in 166 appearances for Leeds United.

His goals-to-games ratio, plus the fact that LUFC were plying their trade at the highest level at the time, demonstrates that the all-action Australian was one of the club's most prolific marksmen of the modern era.

Viduka formed an impressive strike partnership with Alan Smith as Leeds United competed at the top end of the Premier League and in the Champions League too. Fondly remembered for scoring all four goals at Elland Road in a 4-3 Premier League victory over Liverpool in November 2000 - he also netted a hat-trick in a 6-1 romp away to Charlton Athletic in 2002/03 and scored the winning goal at Arsenal which effectively saved Leeds United from relegation.

# LUFC HEROES

## MARK VIDUKA

## HEADERS

A good number of Mark Viduka's Leeds goals came from headers. A real threat in the air, Viduka had the power to out-jump defenders and then use his head to direct the ball past the 'keeper and into the net. Once the ball was in and around the six-yard box and in the air there was always a good chance he would head it home.

## ENCOURAGEMENT

As the focal point of the attack, Viduka could be relied upon to advise and encourage teammates to play the ball into areas where he could be most effective and cause danger to the opposition.

## GOALS

Although a fair amount of Viduka's impressive 72 goals for Leeds came from headers, he was pretty lethal with a trusty right foot too. With the ability to take shots first time or while on the run - when Viduka pulled the trigger with his right foot it rarely let him down.

## CHEST CONTROL

As a strong centre-forward who led the LUFC attack so well, Mark Viduka was blessed with a great ability to play with his back to goal and take the ball under control on his chest. He could then hold up play while others arrived in support or lay the ball off to a teammate.

# RECORD POINTS HAUL

**Not only did Leeds United secure promotion to the Premier League by winning the Sky Bet Championship title in 2019/20 but Marcelo Bielsa's men also set a new club record for points won during a league campaign.**

After missing out in the Play-Offs in 2018/19, Leeds left nothing to chance in 2019/20 as they stormed their way to the title with a 93-point haul. So superior to the rest of Championship, Leeds' 93 points saw them finish the season a whopping ten points clear of runners-up West Bromwich Albion.

# MOST INTERNATIONAL CAPS

**South African central defender Lucas Radebe currently holds the record as Leeds United's most capped international player.**

The former LUFC captain, who joined the club from Kaizer Chiefs in 1994, played in 256 games for Leeds before retiring in 2005. During that lengthy period at Elland Road, Radebe won 58 of his 70 caps for South Africa and captained his country to the World Cup finals in 1998 and 2002. Ironically his final international game came against England in May 2003.

# RECORD APPEARANCE MAKER

**A loyal one-club servant, central defender Jack Charlton amassed a club record 773 appearances for Leeds United.**

Charlton played the first of his 773 games for the club when he debuted against Doncaster Rovers in April 1953. Across a playing career that spanned 20 years, Charlton enjoyed a clean sweep of domestic success with Leeds winning the First Division title, FA Cup, League Cup and Charity Shield. He was also twice a Fairs Cup winner and a member of England's 1966 World Cup winning team. A colossal character in the history of Leeds United, Jack Charlton sadly died on 10 July 2020, aged 85.

# RECORD MAKERS

**A selection of players, games, facts and figures which all shape the club's proud history.**

As we all know there are few better places to be than inside a packed Elland Road and helping cheer Leeds United on to victory.

The record attendance for a Leeds United game at Elland Road was recorded back in the 1966/67 season when LUFC hosted Sunderland in an FA Cup fifth round replay. Having played out a 1-1 draw at Roker Park, a crowd of 57,892 witnessed a second 1-1 draw on 15 March 1967. Leeds eventually won through to the sixth round following a 2-1 victory in a second replay which was played at Hull City's former home of Boothferry Park.

## RECORD ATTENDANCE

## YOUNGEST PLAYER

Leeds United legend Peter Lorimer enjoyed two spells at Elland Road and took the mantle of becoming the club's youngest player when he made his debut in a Second Division match at home to Southampton on 29 September 1962 – he was aged just 15 years and 289 days old.

Few who attended that 1-1 draw with the Saints would have predicted that Lorimer would go on to be the club's greatest-ever goalscorer. The Scot netted an incredible 238 goals for Leeds and is both the club's record marksman and youngest player. A true Leeds great, Peter Lorimer sadly passed away on 20 March 2021 at the age of 74.

# 2021/22 SQUAD

## 15 STUART DALLAS

**POSITION:** Midfielder

**DOB:** 19/04/1991

**COUNTRY:** Northern Ireland

Northern Ireland international Stuart Dallas was ever-present in Leeds United's thrilling return to Premier League action in 2020/21.

A truly remarkable season saw Dallas continue to flourish in a variety of roles under the flexible coaching of Marcelo Bielsa. He scored eight goals and ended the campaign by landing both the club's Player of the Season award and also the Goal of the Season accolade too. The latter award being in respect of his late winner away to champions elect Manchester City in April 2021.

## 19 RODRIGO

**POSITION:** Forward

**DOB:** 06/03/1991

**COUNTRY:** Spain

Leeds United confirmed the signing of Spain international forward Rodrigo for a club record fee ahead of their eagerly-anticipated return to Premier League action in the summer of 2020.

Signed from Valencia, the 30-year-old front man netted seven Premier League goals from 14 starts in his debut campaign at Elland Road including a brace in Leeds' 4-0 away win at Burnley in May 2021.

## 20 DANIEL JAMES

**POSITION:** Midfielder

**DOB:** 10/11/1997

**COUNTRY:** Wales

Flying Wales winger Daniel James joined Leeds United from Premier League rivals Manchester United on the final day of the 2021 summer transfer window.

The Wales international, who began his career at Swansea City, agreed a five-year contract at Elland Road. James did in fact come close to joining Leeds United back in 2018/19 and supporters will be thrilled to finally see his lighting pace in action in a Leeds United shirt.

# IMPOSSIBLE Footy Decisions

**Would you rather...**

have to play the rest of your football games in 35 degree heat or a blizzard?

**Would you rather...**

have Patrick Bamford's ability to score goals or Illan Meslier's ability to save them?

**Would you rather...**

have a pause button or a rewind button for your life?

**Would you rather...**

have unlimited battery life on all your devices or free wifi wherever you go?

**Would you rather...**

run 100 laps of the pitch or complete 200 burpees?

**Would you rather...**

score the FA Cup final winning goal against Manchester United in your only game for Leeds United or play 300 games for LUFC in League One?

**Would you rather...**

be remembered for a terrible footy howler or be forgotten completely?

**Would you rather...**

sell your best player to the Red Devils for £50m or sell him abroad for £20m?

**Would you rather...**

have to take a penalty against Illan Meslier or have Tyler Roberts take a penalty against you?

**Would you rather...**

sit right at the back during a game or have the best seats in the stadium, but not be allowed to eat, drink or use the bathroom?

Would you rather...

**be the star in League Two Or a squad player in the Premier League?**

Would you rather...

## Leeds United win the FA Cup or England win the World Cup?

Would you rather...

*your match superstition be wearing the same socks for a season Or the same underwear for a month?*

Would you rather...

**lose on television or win with nobody watching?**

Would you rather...

have a long, average playing career or have a short, fantastic career cut short by injury?

Would you rather...

lose to Man United twice and finish top or beat them twice and finish bottom?

Would you rather...

**clean the dressing room toilet with your toothbrush or the floor with your tongue?**

Would you rather...

## play only five minutes for Leeds United or win the Premier League with Manchester United?

Would you rather...

have to wear every shirt inside out or every pair of pants backwards?

Would you rather...

**give up your mobile phone for a month or bathing for a month?**

Would you rather...

be alone all your life or surrounded by Manchester United supporters?

**Would you rather... play for Leeds United and always lose Or sit on the bench and LUFC always Win?**

Would you rather...

the half-time menu got rid of pies or pop?

Would you rather...

become a legendary manager or a legendary player?

**A loyal one-club servant, right-back Gary Kelly made over 500 appearances for Leeds United.**

Having made his Leeds debut in 1992, Kelly became a mainstay of the team until 2007, operating predominately at right-back but also in a midfield role on occasions if called upon.

His longevity at Elland Road saw him witness a host of ups and downs at club level while also winning 52 caps for the Republic of Ireland and appearing in the World Cup finals of 1994 and 2002. A real fans' favourite, Kelly is the only Leeds player to make more than 500 appearances for the club outside of the Don Revie era.

# LUFCHEROES

## GARY KELLY

## RALLYING CALL

Often handed the captain's armband, Kelly's ability to lead and inspire his teammates was there for all to see. Always there with an encouraging call to those around him, Kelly led by example and was never afraid to let players know if standards had dropped.

## PASSING SKILLS

Comfortable with the ball at his feet, Kelly was an accomplished ball-playing defender who could always be relied upon to bring the ball out of defence and help the side turn defence to attack.

## TEMPERAMENT

Often faced with containing dangerous wingers, Gary Kelly had the perfect mindset for defending. He very rarely lost concentration and always kept his cool. In the heat of any on-field duel, Kelly kept his mind on the task in hand and more often than not came out on top in one-on-one situations.

## QUICK ON HIS HEELS

Gary Kelly was always alive and alert to danger and when it occurred he was quick on his heels to track and tackle opponents. Not only was he swift over the ground but he was also quick to leap and win headed duels too.

# 2000/01

**Leeds United partnered with kit manufacturer Nike at the start of the 2000/01 season and donned a shirt that has since become a real fans' favourite.**

It was the simplicity and all-white nature of the strip that made it such a hit with supporters. The white shirt had a smart v-neck collar with a very thin blue and yellow trim, a design feature that was then repeated on the cuffs. The club crest, Nike motif and sponsor's branding were all housed on the chest area.

The white shorts had a subtle blue and yellow trim on the side panels and also carried the club crest and manufacturer's logo on the front. This kit's theme was completed with white socks which had a small blue and yellow element added to the top together with the Nike branding.

## DRESSED TO IMPRESS

**Under the management of David O'Leary, Leeds United enjoyed a memorable 2000/01 campaign as the side finished fourth in the Premier League and reached the Champions League semi-finals.**

Striker Mark Viduka topped the scoring charts with 22 goals in all competitions while Leeds enhanced their defensive options with the £18M signing of Rio Ferdinand from West Ham United. The fourth-place finish ensured UEFA Cup football at Elland Road for 2001/02.

## HE WORE IT WELL

**Attacking midfielder Lee Bowyer enjoyed an outstanding 2000/01 at Elland Road and netted six goals in the club's superb run to the Champions League semi-finals.**

Boyer scored a memorable late winner to defeat AC Milan at Elland Road, a brace in the 6-0 demolition of Besiktas and then also opened the scoring against Barcelona. Another late Bowyer strike secured a home win over Anderlecht before he opened the scoring in a thrilling 3-3 draw with Lazio at Elland Road.

In their second season as Leeds United's kit manufacturer, Macron made a number of changes to the club's home kit for the 2009/10 season.

A mainly all-white shirt had a collar added which was enhanced with a thin blue edging. The shirt then had a blue panel running down the left-hand side from the shoulder to the bottom of the shirt. Next to the blue panel was a very thin yellow panel which also ran from the shoulder to the base of the shirt. The club crest, manufacturer's name and sponsor's branding were then housed on the traditional chest area of the shirt. The shirt's sleeves were then completed with a small neat section of blue and yellow piping.

The theme of the blue and yellow panel on the left-hand side of the shirt was then continued on the white shorts, which also carried the club's crest and manufacturer's name. In keeping with the shirt and shorts, the white socks also carried the blue and yellow stripe design down the sides.

### DRESSED TO IMPRESS

**Leeds United ended a three-season stint in League One as Simon Grayson guided the club to promotion as League One runners-up in 2009/10.**

This success was the club's first promotion-winning campaign in 20 years and it went right down to the wire with Leeds having to come from behind to defeat Bristol Rovers in front of a crowd of 38,234 at Elland Road on the final day of the season.

### HE WORE IT WELL

**Jermaine Beckford fired home the goals that won Leeds promotion in 2009/10. The ace marksman netted 31 times in all competitions - 25 in League One including the goal that sealed promotion at home to Bristol Rovers.**

Beckford also netted the only goal of the game as Leeds pulled off an incredible FA Cup third round victory over bitter rivals Manchester United at Old Trafford.

## 2009/10

# ALL KITTED OUT

## 21 PASCUL STRUIJK

**POSITION:** Defender

**DOB:** 11/08/1999

**COUNTRY:** Netherlands

Pascul Struijk joined Leeds United from Ajax in January 2018. A left-footed central defender, Struijk has had to be patient in his pursuit of first-team football at Elland Road.

He debuted in December 2019 as LUFC overcame Hull City at home and made five first-team appearances in the club's 2019/20 Championship title-winning campaign. He made his Premier League bow in the opening-day thriller with Liverpool at Anfield and went on to feature in 26 other top-flight fixtures in 2020/21.

## 22 JACK HARRISON

**POSITION:** Midfielder

**DOB:** 20/11/1996

**COUNTRY:** England

After spending three seasons with Leeds United on separate season-long loan deals from Manchester City, midfielder Jack Harrison put pen to paper on a permanent deal at Elland Road in July 2021.

Having featured in every league game in 2019/20 as Leeds United won the Sky Bet Championship title, Harrison played in all bar two of the club's Premier League matches last season. He netted eight goals last season and is sure to be one of the first names on Marcelo Bielsa's teamsheet during the 2021/22 campaign.

## 2021/22 SQUAD

### 23 KALVIN PHILLIPS

**POSITION:** Midfielder

**DOB:** 02/12/1995

**COUNTRY:** England

Kalvin Phillips followed up an outstanding 2020/21 Premier League season for Leeds United with a series of sensational performances for England in the Euro 2020 finals.

Phillips made 29 Premier League appearances last season and was on target in the final-day victory over West Bromwich Albion. The all-action midfield dynamo then played in all seven of the Three Lions' Euro 2020 games as Gareth Southgate's side ended the tournament as runners-up.

One of a player's greatest assets is the ability to win the ball. The following exercise can be used to improve a player's tackling abilities.

# TACKLING

# SOCCER SKILLS

## EXERCISE

Set up a 10m x 20m grid.

**In this two-on-two exercise, the aim of the game is to score a goal by taking the ball past the two opposing defenders, to the end line, and stand on the ball. The defenders just have to stop them.**

As well as producing plenty of opportunities for the defenders to tackle, this session will test the defenders' abilities to work together, and communicate.

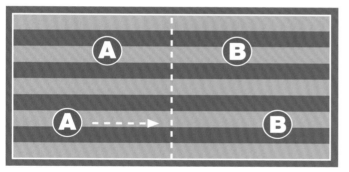

## Key Factors

1.  **Be patient - do not dive in.**

2.  **Stay on your feet if possible.**

3.  **Time the tackle with bodyweight behind it.**

4.  **Be determined to win it.**

The reason that great players win so many tackles is not just because they know how to tackle and have good technique, it is because they have big hearts and are determined to win their challenges on the pitch.

# ODDBALLS

**1**

C
B
D
A

ANSWER Sunderland

**2**

B
A
C
D
1898

ANSWER Portsmouth

Three of the four pictures in each football represent a Premier League or Football League club, can you figure out the football club as well as the odd one out?

**3**

C
B
A
D

ANSWER Arsenal

**4**

C
B
A
D

FOOTBALL CLUB

ANSWER

**5**

B
A
C
D

ANSWER

ANSWERS ON PAGE 62

**6**
- A
- B
- C
- D
- Crystal Palace

**7**
- A
- B
- C
- D
- Spurs

**8**
- A
- B
- C
- D
- Reading

**9**
- A
- B
- C
- D
- Birmingham City
- FOOTBALL CLUB

**10**
- A
- B
- C
- D
- West Ham

LUFC

1905

# GOAL
## OF THE SEASON

## STUART DALLAS
### V MANCHESTER CITY · APRIL 2021

**Stuart Dallas capped off a tremendous 2020/21 campaign when he followed up his Player of the Year accolade by collecting the club's Goal of the Season award too. Dallas netted an impressive eight Premier League goals as Leeds United took the top flight by storm, ending an exceptional campaign with 59 points and a ninth-placed finish.**

It was Dallas' seventh goal of the season - a memorable late winner against champions-elect Manchester City at the Etihad Stadium in April that won him the Goal of the Season award on an afternoon when the Northern Ireland international became Leeds' two-goal hero.

Having earned a valuable point against Pep Guardiola's men when the two sides met at Elland Road in October, Leeds went one better by securing all three points at the Etihad. It was Dallas who put Leeds in front when he sent a low shot past City 'keeper Ederson and in off of the post just three minutes before the break.

Despite returning to the dressing room with a one-goal advantage at half-time, Leeds still faced an uphill struggle in the second half as they took on Guardiola's free-scoring superstars with ten men after skipper Liam Cooper was dismissed in first-half injury-time.

Leeds withstood a barrage of City attacks but kept their goal intact until Ferran Torres struck a 76th-minute equaliser. A man down and having just conceded an equaliser, it looked like being a testing final 14 minutes for LUFC if they were to hang on for a point. However, against all the odds it was Leeds - inspired by Dallas - who conjured up the game's winning goal. A minute into injury-time and Dallas ran on to Ezgjan Alioski's beautifully weighted through-ball and fired past Ederson from the edge of the area. The goal was Dallas' second of the game and capped off a sensational and surprise victory.

Leeds United were great entertainers throughout their 2020/21 Premier League adventure and there really were some cracking effort's among the 62 league goals they scored. However for sheer drama there was not much to compete with Dallas' second strike against the runaway leaders - a goal clearly worthy of the club's Goal of the Season award.

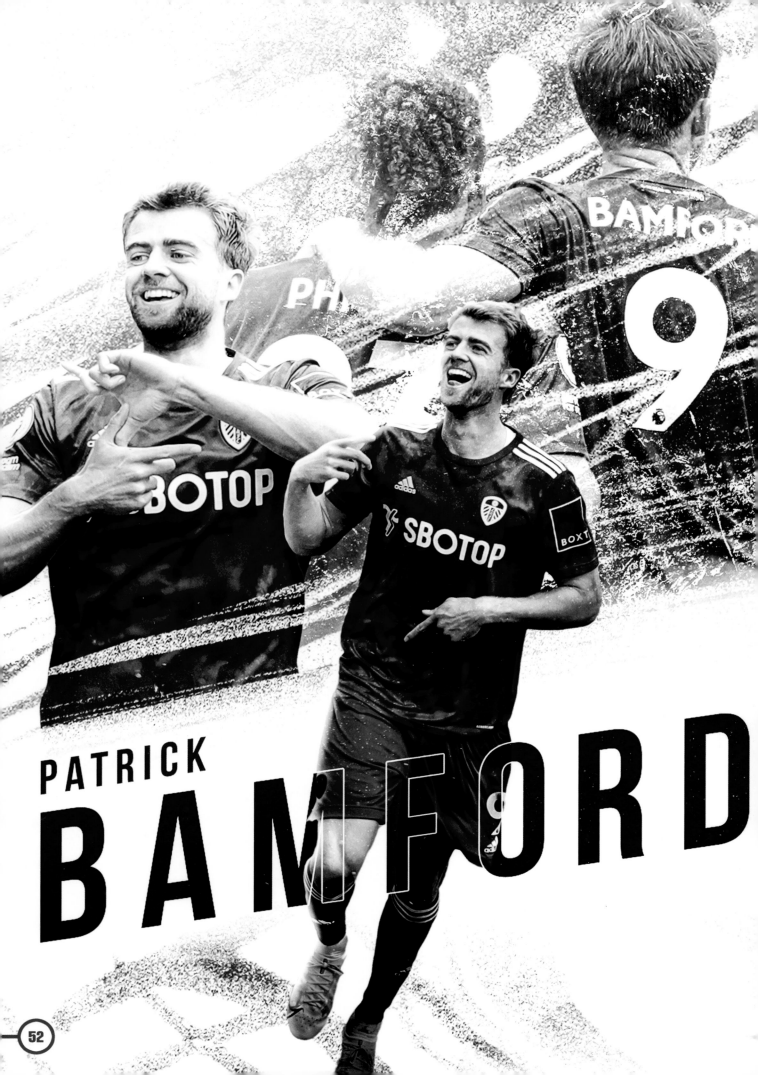

PATRICK
BAMFORD

**COLOUR LIAM COOPER**

## 30 JOE GELHARDT

| POSITION: | Forward |
| DOB: | 04/04/2002 |
| COUNTRY: | England |

Leeds United signed highly-promising teenage forward Joe Gelhardt from Wigan Athletic in August 2020.

A powerful left-footed forward, who displays great dribbling skills, Gelhardt agreed a four-year contract when he arrived at Elland Road. After bursting on to the first-team scene with Wigan as a 16-year-old, Gelhardt has won international caps with England at U16, U17, U18 and U20 level.

## 43 MATEUSZ KLICH

| POSITION: | Midfielder |
| DOB: | 13/06/1990 |
| COUNTRY: | Poland |

One of a clutch of Leeds players to feature in the Euro 2020 finals, Polish midfielder Mateusz Klich played in all three of his country's group games following an excellent debut campaign in the Premier League.

The 31-year-old has become a regular face in the LUFC side in the Bielsa-era at Leeds and marked his Premier League debut with a goal against Liverpool. In total he weighed in with four goals from his 35 Premier League outings in 2020/21.

# 2021/22 SQUAD

## 46 JAMIE SHACKLETON

**POSITION:** Midfielder

**DOB:** 08/10/1999

**COUNTRY:** England

A product of the club's Academy system, Leeds-born Jamie Shackleton first joined the club at the age of seven.

After progressing though the youth ranks, Shackleton made his first debut when he appeared from the bench in the Whites' 4-1 victory over Derby County in August 2018. With the ability to operate in central midfield or at right-back, he agreed a new four-year contract at the club in August 2020 and made 13 appearances in the Premier League last season.

# 1. WHO AM I?

I joined Leeds United from Sheffield Wednesday

I moved to Elland Road in 1991

I'm remembered for scoring a vital goal in the club's 1991/92 title triumph

I played 76 league games for Leeds, scoring three goals

I left Elland Road in 1994 and headed to East Anglia

# 3. WHO AM I?

I was born in Morley in 1988

I began my career with the Leeds United Academy

I made my first-team debut for Leeds in a League Cup tie with Barnet

I scored my first Leeds goal against a club I would later play for

I played in Leeds' memorable FA Cup victory away to Manchester United in 2010

# GUESS WHO

# 2. WHO AM I?

I was born in South America in December 1983

I was signed for Leeds by Gary McAllister

I marked my league debut for Leeds with an early goal

I scored 15 league goals in Leeds' 2009/10 League One promotion-winning season

I made over 200 appearances for Leeds before leaving the club in 2013

## 4. WHO AM I?

I began my career with West Ham United

My transfer fee when joining Leeds United set a new club record

I was part of the Leeds team that reached the Champions League semi-finals

I made a controversial move to join a major rival in 2002

My playing career saw me win over 80 caps for England

Can you identify these six former Elland Road men from the clues given? Good luck!

## 5. WHO AM I?

I was born in Chesterfield in 1960

I began my long playing career at Elland Road

I had two separate spells as Leeds player

I was capped by England at U21 level during my first spell with the club

I was a member of the club's 1991/92 First Division title-winning team

## 6. WHO AM I?

I was born in Spain in 1985

I first sampled the English game with a spell at Swansea City

I first joined Leeds on loan before agreeing a permanent move to Yorkshire

I was voted Leeds United's Player of the Season on three consecutive occasions

I was a Championship title winner with Leeds in 2019/20

ANSWERS ON PAGE 62

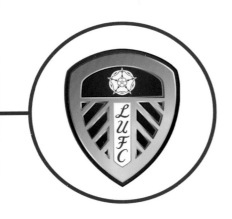

A real Elland Road favourite, experienced Scottish international Gordon Strachan is the only player, other than Billy Bremner, to lift a major trophy for Leeds United.

Always remembered for his stunning Elland Road strike against Leicester City in 1990 en route to promotion from the Second Division, Strachan then skippered the club to the First Division title just two years later.

Strachan was an inspired signing by Howard Wilkinson in March 1989. The 33-year-old was an outstanding performer on the pitch who thrived on the responsibility of the captaincy and proved to be a real role model for teammates.

# LUFC HEROES

## GORDON STRACHAN

### EYE FOR AN OPENING

Not only was Strachan extremely comfortable on the ball but he also showed great vision and awareness on the pitch. He appeared to have the perfect eye for a quick pass to help Leeds mount another attack.

### QUICK FEET

Naturally blessed with exceptional close control and dribbling skills, Strachan had the ability to jinx his way past opponents and into dangerous areas. Always indentified as the dangerman, Strachan proved to be a tricky player for opposition to get to grips with.

### INTELLIGENCE

A player's football intelligence is often spoken about and Strachan had it in abundance. He had the skill of making time on the ball, orchestrating the pattern of play and playing creative forward balls. He also had that ability of knowing the runs a teammate would make and skill to find them with the minimum of fuss.

### ADVICE

Strachan used his vast experience and knowledge gained from playing at the top level for club and country to help nurture and inspire the younger players in the Leeds squad.

# FAST FORWARD

Do your predictions for 2021/22 match our own?...

### PREMIER LEAGUE TOP SCORER
## Jamie Vardy

*Mo Salah*

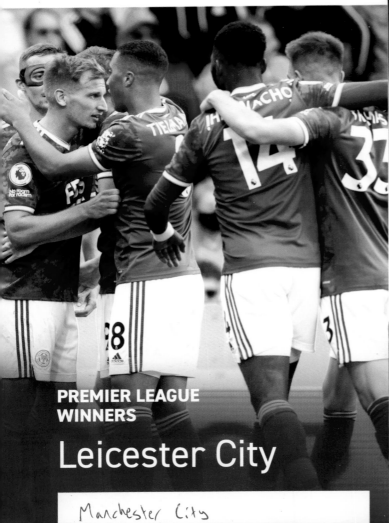

### PREMIER LEAGUE WINNERS
## Leicester City

*Manchester City*

### PREMIER LEAGUE RUNNERS-UP
## Chelsea

*Liverpool*

### FA CUP WINNERS
## Leeds United

*Spurs*

### FA CUP RUNNERS-UP
## Watford

*Wolves*

### LEAGUE CUP WINNERS
## Arsenal

*Chelsea*

### LEAGUE CUP RUNNERS-UP
## Leicester City

*Arsenal*

## CHAMPIONSHIP WINNERS
Fulham

Fulham

## CHAMPIONSHIP RUNNERS-UP
Derby County

Bournemouth

## CHAMPIONSHIP PLAY-OFF WINNERS
Reading

West Brom

## CHAMPIONSHIP TOP SCORER
Ivan Cavaleiro

Mitrovic

## LEEDS UNITED TOP SCORER
Patrick Bamford

Raphinha

## CHAMPIONS LEAGUE WINNERS
Barcelona

Manchester City

## CHAMPIONS LEAGUE RUNNERS-UP
Real Madrid

Bayern

## LEEDS UNITED PLAYER OF THE YEAR
Luke Ayling

Raphinha

## EUROPA LEAGUE WINNERS
West Ham United

Lyon

## EUROPA LEAGUE RUNNERS-UP
Lazio

Napoli

# ANSWERS

## PAGE 11
### SOCCER SEARCH

Bicycle Kick.

## PAGE 14
### CLASSIC FANTASTIC

## PAGE 26
### GUESS THE CLUB

1. Newcastle United. 2. Wigan Athletic. 3. Burnley.
4. Charlton Athletic. 5. Coventry City. 6. AFC Wimbledon.
7. Liverpool. 8. Millwall. 9.Wolverhampton Wanderers.
10. Nottingham Forest.

## PAGE 48
### ODD BALLS

1. Sunderland, C. 2. Portsmouth, C. 3. Arsenal, B.
4. Crewe Alexandra, A. 5. Queens Park Rangers, C.
6. Crystal Palace, B. 7. Tottenham Hotspur, B.
8. Reading, B. 9. Birmingham City, C.
10. West Ham United, D.

## PAGE 56
### GUESS WHO?

1. Jon Newsome. 2. Luciano Becchio. 3. Jonny Howson.
4. Rio Ferdinand. 5. John Lukic. 6. Pablo Hernandez.